The Monster

Written by Paul Shipton
Illustrated by Anni Axworthy

Joe and his sister Jade liked the snow.
They were going to the hill to play.

"Do not go to the hill!" said an old man.
"Why not?" asked Jade.

"The Snow Monster's home is near there," the old man told them.

"Who is the Snow Monster?" asked Joe.
"He is a beast with long hair," said the
old man.

"The Snow Monster's teeth grow sharp,"
said the old man. "His nose is as red
as glowing coal."

"The Snow Monster is only a story,"
said Jade.
Jade and Joe strode away.

Soon it was snowing again.
A cold wind was blowing.
"We have to go home," said Joe.

Just then, there was a bellow from
the trees.
Both children froze in fear.

A light was glowing.
A big shadow came nearer ...

Yikes! The Snow Monster!
He showed his rows of sharp teeth.

"We HAVE to go home!" said Joe again.
But Jade spoke to the monster, "Hello."

"HELLO," he bellowed.
"Why are you so angry?" asked Jade.

The Snow Monster groaned. "I have grown up on this hill. But ...

... my toes are FREEZING! It is too cold!"
"Come home with us," said the children.
"We can make hot toast."

The children strolled down the hill with the Snow Monster.
"Hello," they said to the old man.